READABOUT
Directions

This edition 2003

Franklin Watts
96 Leonard Street
London EC2A 4XD

Franklin Watts Australia
45-51 Huntley Street
Alexandria
NSW 2015

Copyright © 1992 Franklin Watts

Editor: Ambreen Husain
Design: K and Co

A CIP catalogue record for this book is available
from the British Library.

ISBN 0 7496 5271 3

Printed in Hong Kong

READABOUT
Directions

Text: Henry Pluckrose
Photography: Chris Fairclough

FRANKLIN WATTS
LONDON•SYDNEY

These footprints were
made in sand.
The person who made them
was going to the left.

This person was going to the right.
Why do we need words like 'right' and 'left'?

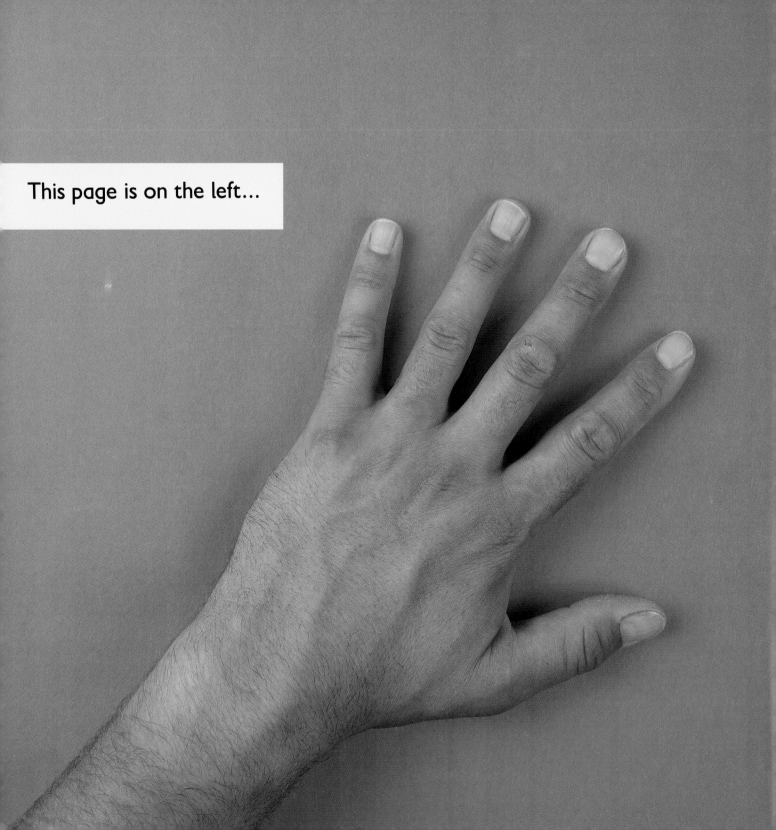

This page is on the left...

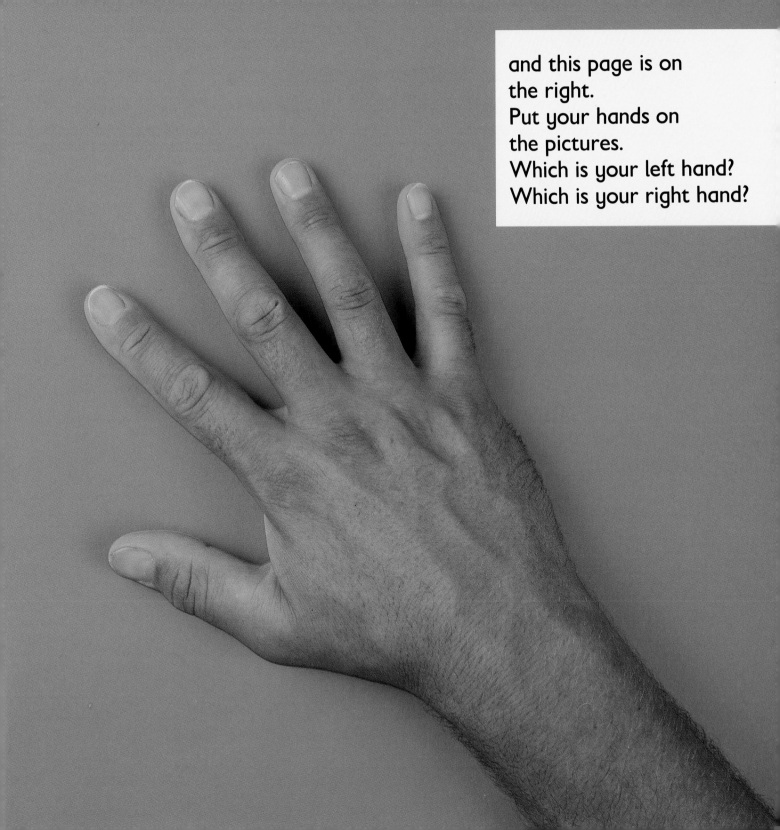

and this page is on
the right.
Put your hands on
the pictures.
Which is your left hand?
Which is your right hand?

Most people use
their right hand to do things
like writing,
threading a needle
or hammering a nail.
Are you right-handed?

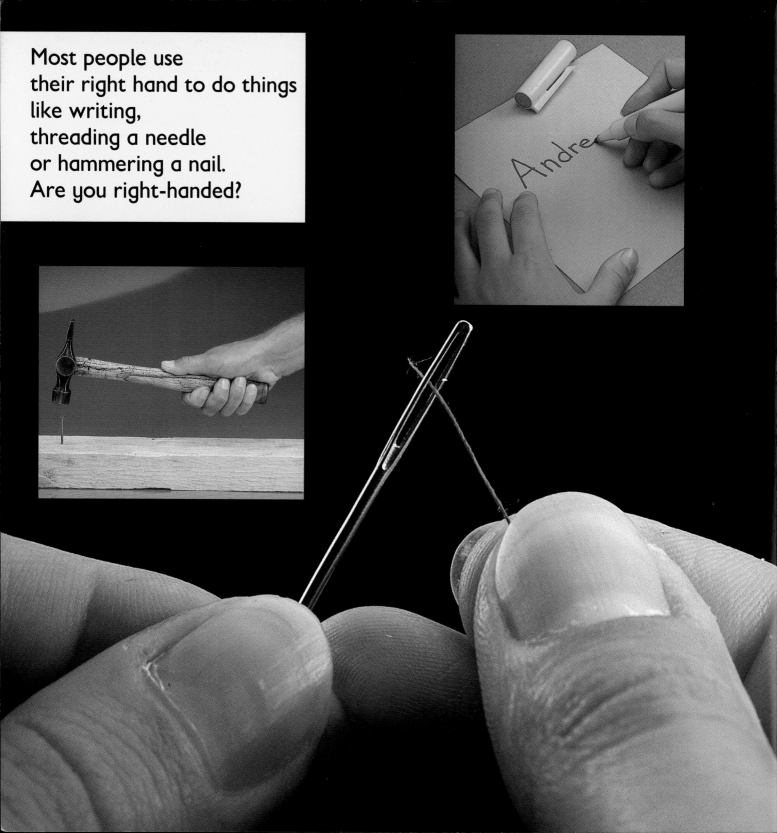

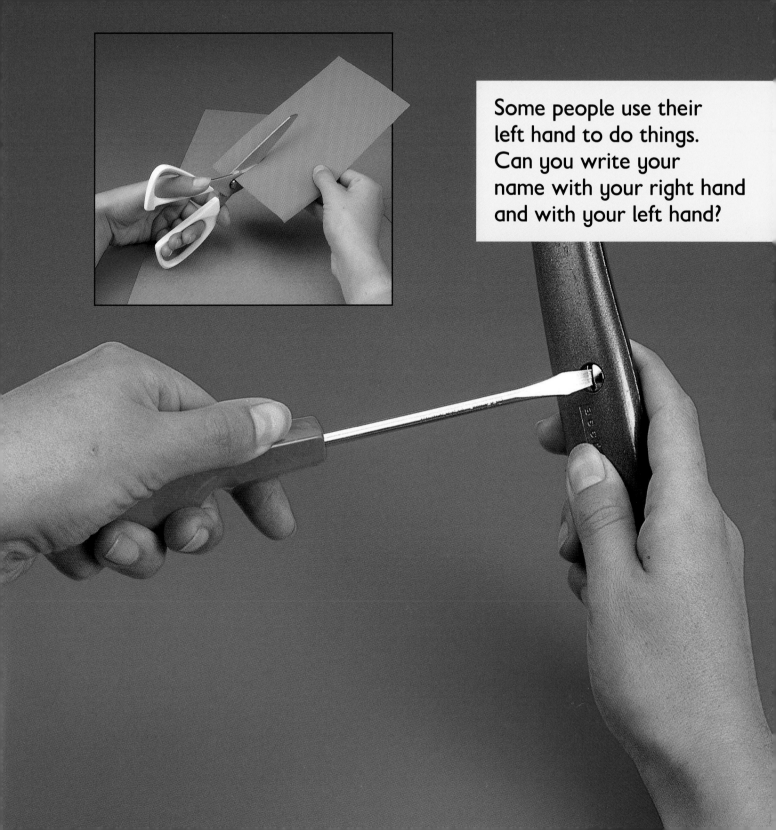

Some people use their left hand to do things. Can you write your name with your right hand and with your left hand?

Are you always sure
which is right and
which is left?
Look at these pictures.
The flag is
in the figure's right hand.

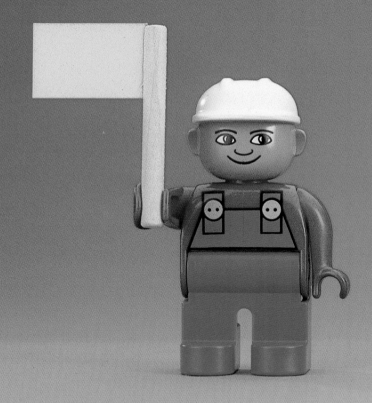

What do you notice
when the figure turns round?

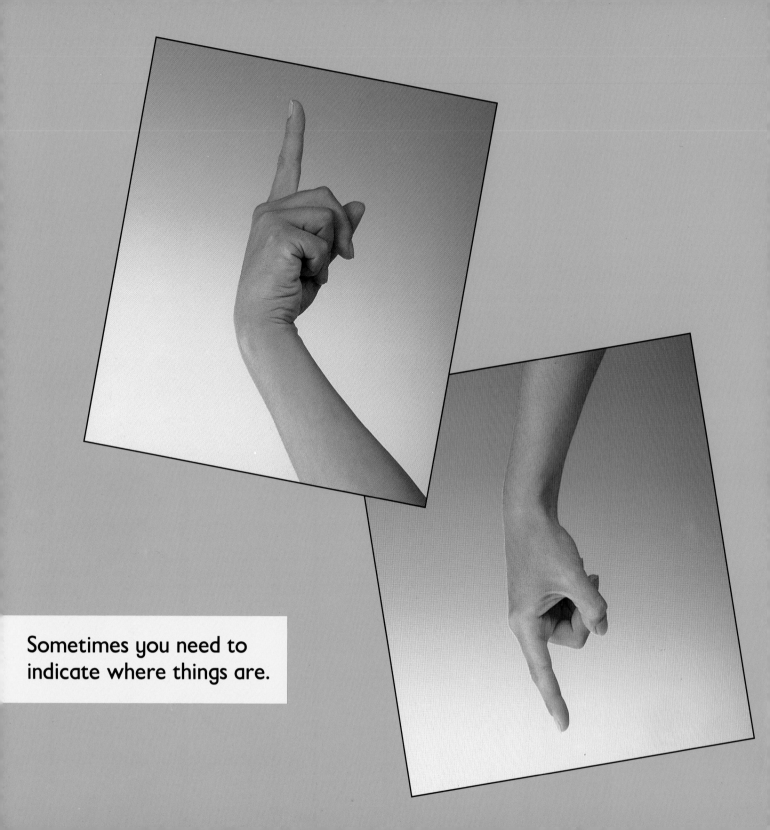

Sometimes you need to
indicate where things are.

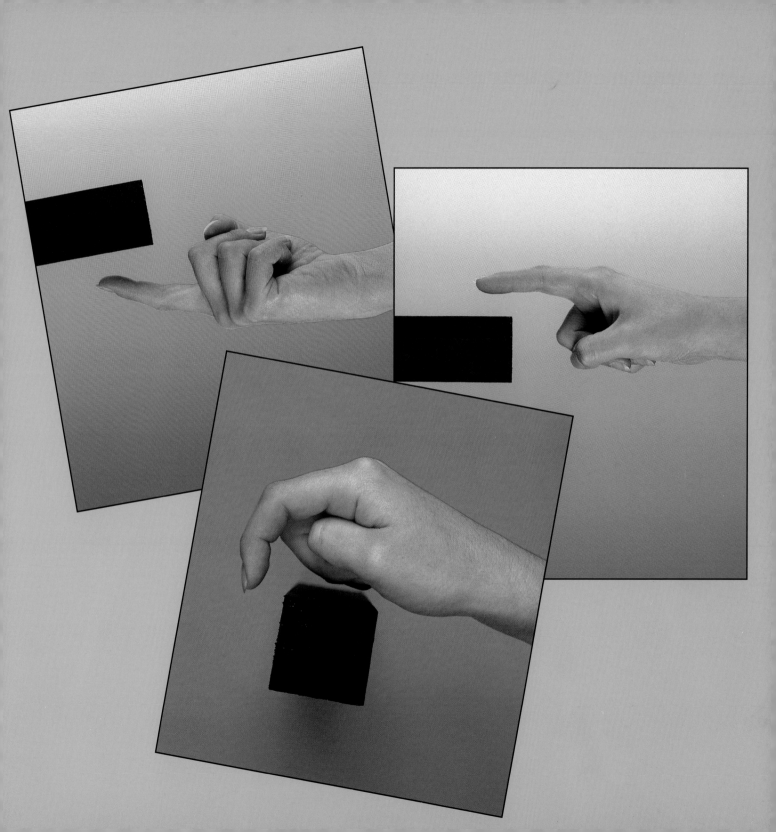

There are signs which tell road users which way to go.

What do these signs
tell the driver
and the cyclist.

Drivers and cyclists often have to share the road with those travelling in the opposite direction. On what side of the road are these cars travelling...

and these?

What else might you need to help you find your way on a long car journey?

D 774

CHAMBRES·HÔTES

D 21

St GRAVE
LA GACILLY

MALANSAC
ALLAIRE

PLEUCADEUC
MALESTROIT

*Parc de
Préhistoire*

La Grêle

Road signs like these tell you where to turn off one road and join another. Which of these signs is pointing to the left?

There are no signs in the sky to help the pilot of an aircraft or marks in the sea to help the captain of a ship.

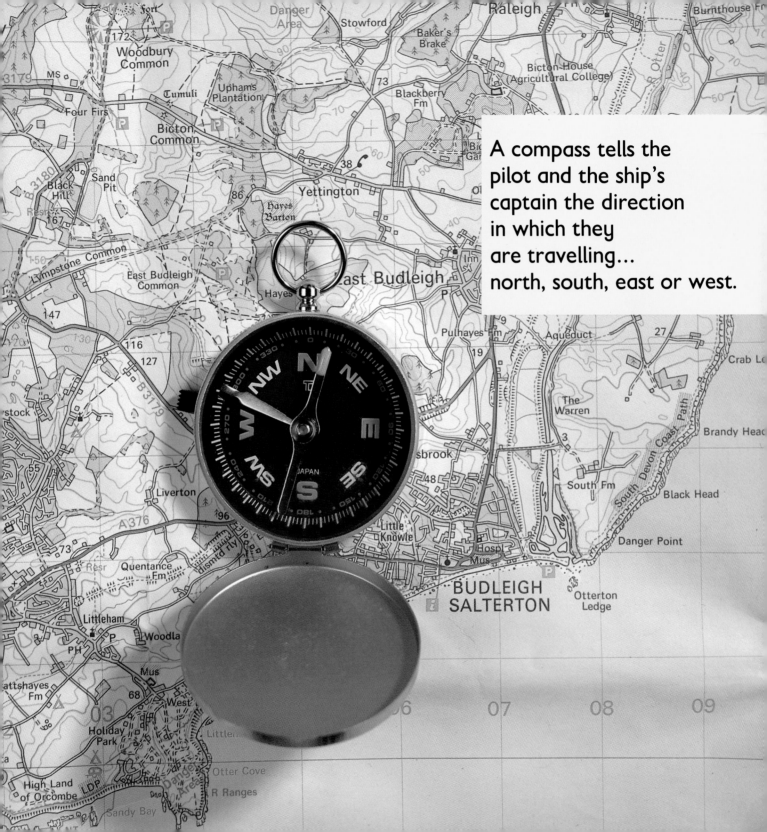

A compass tells the pilot and the ship's captain the direction in which they are travelling... north, south, east or west.

There are other words
we use to explain
where things are.
The toy car runs down
the slope from the top
to the bottom.

The beans can be in the tin,
in the saucepan
or on the plate.
Where are they now?

Everything which has a front
also has a back
and at least two sides.
Front is the opposite of back.
Back is the opposite of front.

Many things have an inside too!

When we move we change
our position.
The puppet could be up
on a seat
looking down...

or down on the floor
looking up.
Up is the opposite of down.
What does opposite mean?

Find the coloured block.
It is inside the bowl
but outside the hoop.
What other things are
outside the hoop?

Some things are always
arranged in a similar way.
What a muddle this is.
Knowing which is left and
which is right makes it
easy to lay the table.

28

What would life be like
without any directions?

About this book

All books which are specially prepared for young children are written to meet the interest of the age group at which they are directed. This may mean presenting an idea in a humorous or unconventional way so that ideas which hitherto have been grasped somewhat hazily are given sharper focus. The books in this series aim to bring into focus some of the elements of life and living which we as adults tend to take for granted.

This book develops and explores an idea using simple text and thought-provoking photographs. The words will encourage questioning and discussion – whether they are read by adult or child. Children enjoy having information books read to them just as much as stories and poetry. The younger child may ignore the written words … pictures play an important part in learning, particularly if they encourage talk and visual discrimination.

Young children acquire much information in an incidental, almost random fashion. Indeed, they learn much just by being alive! The adult who uses books like this one needs to be sympathetic and understanding of the young child's intellectual development.
It offers a particular way of looking, an approach to questioning which will result in talk, rather than 'correct' one word answers.

Henry Pluckrose